A Beginning-to-Read Book

BIG FEELINGS

FEELING BRAVE

by Mary Lindeen

NORWOOD HOUSE PRESS

DEAR CAREGIVER, The *Beginning to Read* Big Feelings books support children's social and emotional learning (SEL). SEL has been proven to promote not only the development of self-awareness, responsibility, and positive relationships but also academic achievement.

Current research reveals that the part of the brain that manages emotion is directly connected to the part of the brain that is used in cognitive tasks such as problem solving, logic, reasoning, and critical thinking—all of which are at the heart of learning.

SEL is also directly linked to what are referred to as 21st Century Skills: collaboration, communication, creativity, and critical thinking. The books included in this SEL series offer an early start to help children build the competencies they need for success in school and life.

In each of these books, young children will learn how to recognize, name, and manage their own feelings while learning that everyone shares the same emotions. This helps them develop social competencies that will benefit them in their relationships with others, which in turn contributes to their success in school. As they read, children will also practice early reading skills by reading sight words and content vocabulary.

The reinforcements in the back of each book will help you determine how well your child understands the concepts in the book, provide different ideas for your child to practice fluency, and suggest books and websites for additional reading.

The most important part of the reading experience with these books—and all others—is for your child to have fun and enjoy reading and learning!

Sincerely,

Mary Lindeen

Mary Lindeen, Author

Norwood House Press
For more information about Norwood House Press please visit our website at www.norwoodhousepress.com or call 866-565-2900.
© 2022 Norwood House Press. Beginning-to-Read™ is a trademark of Norwood House Press.
All rights reserved. No part of this book may be reproduced or utilized in any form or
by any means without written permission from the publisher.

Editor: Judy Kentor Schmauss   **Designer**: Sara Radka

Photo Credits: Getty Images: 1BSG, 3, 1BSG, 5, Alistair Berg, 13, Ariel Skelley, 14, Blue Jean Images, 6, Don Mason, 9, EyeEm/Jesada Wongsa, 18, Image Source, 26, JGI/Tom Grill, 17, Jupiterimages, 25, prostooleh, 22, Ridofranz, cover, 1, SDI Productions, 10; Shutterstock: alexkatkov, 29, Szasz-Fabian Ilka Erika, 21

Library of Congress Cataloging-in-Publication Data has been filed and is available at catalog.loc.gov

Library ISBN: 978-1-68450-819-8   Paperback ISBN: 978-1-68404-669-0

It can be a little scary to try something new.

You might not like it.

Or you might like it a lot!

Are you feeling brave enough to try?

Feeling brave means doing something even when it feels a little scary.

Doing things by yourself can feel scary.

Feeling brave helps you do them anyway.

Asking questions can feel scary.

Feeling brave helps you ask them anyway.

Everyone feels scared sometimes.

And everyone feels brave sometimes, too.

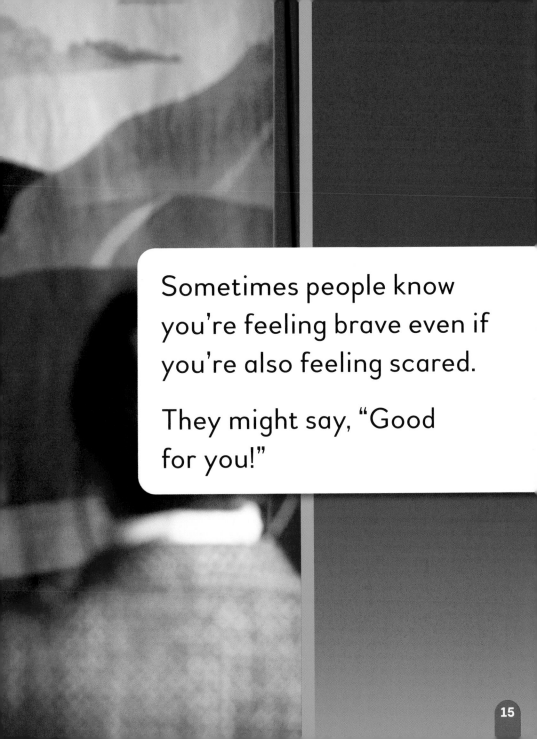

Sometimes people know you're feeling brave even if you're also feeling scared.

They might say, "Good for you!"

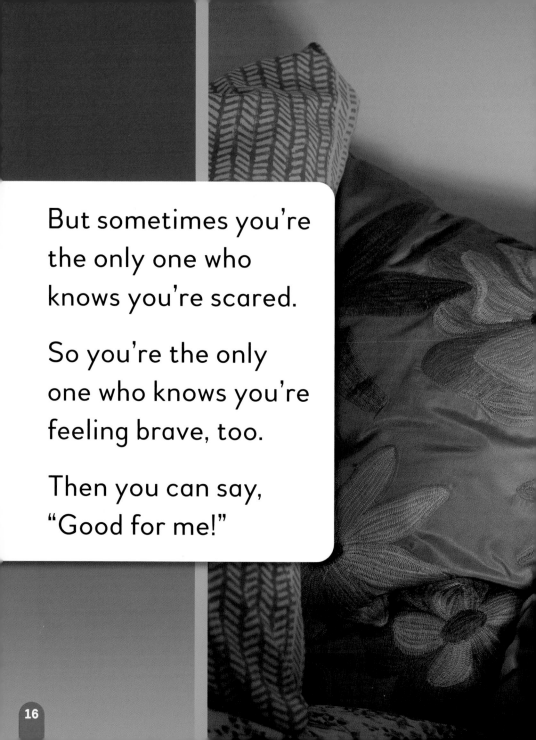

But sometimes you're the only one who knows you're scared.

So you're the only one who knows you're feeling brave, too.

Then you can say, "Good for me!"

Feeling brave
helps you learn
new things.

It helps you
try again, even
when you fail.

Failing can feel scary.

But failing helps us learn what we're doing wrong.

Everyone who fails felt brave enough to try.

You can help
others feel brave.

You can say,
"You've got this!"

Feeling brave also helps you show kindness.

You might feel a little scared to say, "How can I help?"

Or even to say, "I was wrong. I'm sorry."

Feeling brave helps you say those words.

How can you show
you feel brave today?

...READING REINFORCEMENT...

CONNECTING CONCEPTS

CLOSE READING OF NONFICTION TEXT

Close reading helps children comprehend text. It includes reading a text, discussing it with others, and answering questions about it. Use these questions to discuss this book with your child:

1. What does it mean to feel brave?
2. How does feeling brave help us?

Once you have discussed the above questions, ask your child to either draw a picture of someone who is feeling brave or choose one of the children pictured in the book. Then ask the following questions about the child in the drawing or the photo:

1. How can you tell this person might be feeling brave?
2. What might be one reason this person is feeling brave?
3. How would you feel in that situation?
4. Do you ever feel brave? When?
5. When you're feeling a little scared but you want to feel brave, what do you do? How could someone else help you feel more brave?

VOCABULARY AND LANGUAGE SKILLS

As you read the book with your child, make sure he or she understands the vocabulary used. Point to key words and talk about what they mean. Encourage children to sound out new words or to read the familiar words around an unfamiliar word for help reading new words.

FLUENCY

Help your child practice fluency by using one or more of the following activities:

1. Reread the book to your child at least two times while he or she uses a finger to track each word as it is read.

2. Read a line of the book, then reread it as your child reads along with you.

3. Ask your child to go back through the book and read the words he or she knows.

4. Have your child practice reading the book several times to improve accuracy, rate, and expression.

FURTHER READING FOR KIDS

Howarth, Heidi. *What Makes Me Brave?* New York, NY: Sky Pony Press, 2019.

Robertson, Rachel. *Beginners Are Brave*. St. Paul, MN: Redleaf Press, 2019.

Sinarski, Jessica. *Riley the Brave: The Little Cub with Big Feelings!* Philadelphia, PA: Jessica Kingsley Publishers, 2021.

FURTHER READING FOR TEACHERS/CAREGIVERS

The Center for Parenting Education: Kids and Courage
https://centerforparentingeducation.org/library-of-articles/self-esteem/kids-and-courage/

Hey Sigmund: Building Courage in Kids—How to Teach Kids to Be Brave
https://www.heysigmund.com/building-courage-in-kids/

PBS for Parents: Becoming Brave: Help Your Child Move Past Fear
https://www.pbs.org/parents/thrive/becoming-brave-help-your-child-move-past-fear

Feeling Brave uses the 76 words listed below. *High-frequency* words are those words that are used most often in the English language. They are sometimes referred to as sight words because children need to learn to recognize them automatically when they read. *Content* words are any words specific to a particular topic. Regular practice reading these words will enhance your child's ability to read with greater fluency and comprehension.

HIGH-FREQUENCY WORDS

a	good	one	things
again	help(s)	only	this
also	how	or	those
and	I	other(s)	to
are	if	people	too
ask(ing)	it	say	us
be	know(s)	show	was
but	like	so	what
by	little	something	when
can	me	the	who
do(ing)	might	them	word(s)
even	new	then	you
for	not	they	

CONTENT WORDS

anyway	got	scared	wrong
brave	I'm	scary	you're
enough	kindness	sometimes	you've
everyone	learn	sorry	yourself
fail(ing, s)	lot	today	
feel(ing, s)	means	try	
felt	questions	we're	

About the Author

Mary Lindeen is a writer, editor, parent, and former elementary school teacher. She has written more than 100 books for children and edited many more. She specializes in early literacy instruction and books for young readers, especially nonfiction.